UPCYCLE
Your Wardrobe

Mia Führer

UPCYCLE
Your Wardrobe

21 Sewing Projects for Unique, New Fashions

Schiffer
Publishing Ltd

4880 Lower Valley Road • Atglen, PA 19310

Dear Reader,

Do you sometimes feel like this, too?—

You get a last-minute invitation and ask yourself, "What should I wear?" You then stand in front of the well-stocked closet and think: "I have *nothing* to wear!" It's not about wearing just anything; it's about wearing the right thing—and that's not always an easy task.

But it doesn't always have to involve buying a new piece! You can create new garments from fabric leftovers, or even some artificial fur. With the twenty-one projects here, there are no limits to your wardrobe flexibility. Everything here can be sewn quickly…and it's fun! The descriptive photo instructions make it easy to follow the process step by step. Even beginners will be successful with these projects in no time.

There are so many reasons to jazz up your "old" pieces! Let yourself be inspired by this book. You'll find many great ideas to copy, all based on the motto: Upcycle your wardrobe!

Contents

Let's Party!

The simple T-shirt is transformed into a great dress with a chiffon skirt. The spangle edging adds sparkle.

Materials

- one simple T-shirt
- 2 yards polyester chiffon, 50" wide
- spangle edging trim, ⅜" wide. Calculate the length as follows: hip measurement plus about 4" seam allowance, and neckline width plus ¾" seam allowance.

How to do it

Put on the T-shirt and pin it to the desired length. The dress in the photo has a back length of 37". The chiffon skirt itself is 15¾" long, and is made from four panels of fabric.

Place two fabric panels right sides together. Iron the seam allowances open, then stitch along one edge with a long running stitch, ½" wide, then stitch another row ¼" from the first. Take the two threads next to each other on one end of the fabric, and pull together to gather, reducing the width to half the hip measurement, plus an additional 2" for comfort. Repeat with two more panels.

Place the skirt sections right sides together and stitch the side seams. Serge the hem edge, then fold the hem edge over twice, and stitch it with the machine.

Place the chiffon skirt onto the T-shirt right sides together, slightly stretching the shirt's edge, and pin them together.

Stitch up the seam, serge the seam allowances together, and iron them toward the T-shirt.

On the right side, pin on the spangle edging. Stitch along both edges of it, staying close to the edge.

Then stitch the spangle edging onto the neckline in the same way.

Black and White

Give your patterned pullover a new kind of style. The snug (ripped) neckline is replaced with a fashionable V-neck.

Materials

- one pullover-type sweater
- ⅓ yard knit tube fabric, approx. 19¾" wide

How to do it

Put on the pullover and place a pin at the lowest point of the new neckline: in this case, 5½" down.

Measure to locate the front center, and mark it with a basting stitch.

Fold the sweater at the front center. Make sure the shoulder seams are exactly aligned. Pin together, and baste along the new neckline.

Then cut ⅜" away from your basting line.

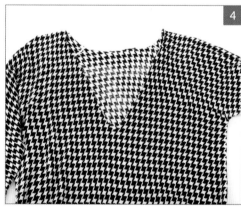

Cut off the old neck ribbing too. ▶

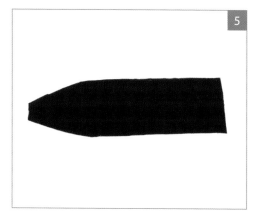

Measure the new neckline and cut the knit tube fabric in two sections (see diagram).

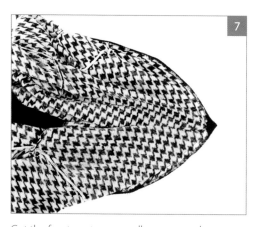

Cut the front center seam allowance to the corner, and place the edges of the pieces over each other.

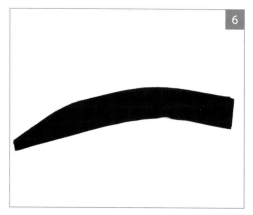

Fold each section in half at the center line and carefully iron into shape. Briefly iron the edge and stretch the outer edge a little bit.

Open up the sections and stitch them together at the back center seam. Iron the seam flat. Place the edges onto the sweater neckline edges, and stitch, slightly stretched (try using pins), onto the neckline.

Trim the seam allowances and iron toward the sweater.

Collar Pattern

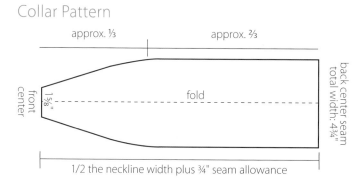

approx. ⅓   approx. ⅔

front center

1⅝"

fold

back center seam total width: 4¾"

1/2 the neckline width plus ¾" seam allowance

Soft and Warm

This knitted vest is missing that special something. Make a fluffy, faux-fur removable collar that snaps onto it.

Materials

- one knitted jacket or vest
- ½ yard faux fur, 60" wide
- ½ yard lining fabric, 58" wide
- plastic snaps, transparent, ½" diameter

How to do it

First make a collar pattern. Place the collar portion of the vest flat along the edge of a piece of paper, and pin it down. Draw along its outer edge to the back center seam. Draw a line from here to the collar's inner edge. Continue the line back to the lower collar edge where you started, adding ¾" to this side's width to accommodate the rolling width.

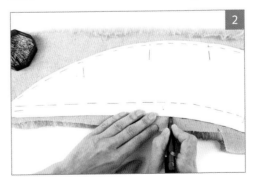

Trace the collar pattern onto the wrong side of the fake fur. Flip the pattern upside down and cut a second piece. Important: make sure that the two collar pieces are symmetrical.

Cut, adding ¼" seam allowance. Try to only cut the fabric with the scissors—pull the fur fibers apart.

Pull the scraps away from the fur pieces. ▶

For the lining, cut off ¼" from the edge of your pattern. Then cut the lining sections to that size, leaving a ¼" seam allowance at the back center.

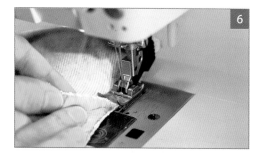

Carefully pulling back the fur fibers with your fingers, stitch the collar pieces together at the back center seam, right sides together.

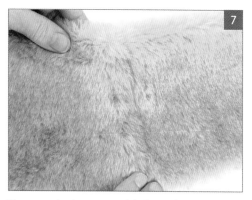

The seam is almost invisible from the outside.

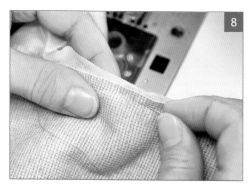

Baste the lining and fur on top of each other, carefully pulling the fur fibers to the inside (with scissors or seam ripper; see photo 6 on page 24). Sew together.

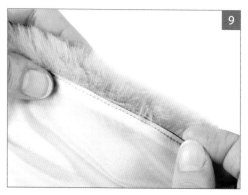

Turn the collar right side out, and stitch closely along the lining edge; the seam allowances are under it. Then pull out the fur fibers with a needle if needed.

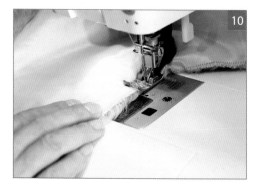

Sew the lining and fur together at the inner edge of the collar using a zigzag stitch.

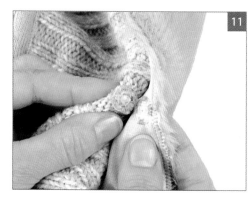

Sew on (or attach with the appropriate snap tool) the snaps, placing them about 4½" apart.

A Beautiful Back

This blouse gets transformed into a summer halter-back top with a lapel collar. Great for a beach party!

Materials

- one blouse
- ½ yard elastic, ⅜" wide

How to do it

Put on the blouse, or place it on a tailor's dummy.

Turn up the collar, and pin along your chosen line. Remove the shirt and baste a line on the front and back sections.

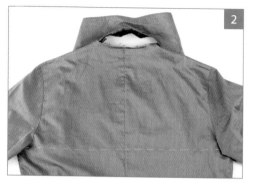

Use a seam ripper or scissors to rip out the collar from the shirt at its back section only, up to the shoulder seams.

Completely remove the sleeves, rip out the shoulder seams, and place the arm openings on top of each other. Draw a line of seam allowance ⅜" away from the basting thread line, and cut along it.

Try on the blouse; you may want to pin it at the back center seam and at the side seams to achieve the best fit. Trim, pin, and stitch.

Iron the seam allowance toward the inside, and stitch the edges.

Sew the edges at the back collar together.

To give the blouse better support at the back, add elastic to the back edge, sewing it on with a zigzag stitch.

Please Cut Up!

The turtleneck collar was too tight at the neck, and a zippered jacket is more versatile and sporty anyway.

Materials

- one turtleneck sweater
- satin ribbon (or binding), 1" wide, as long as the length of the jacket including length of turtleneck and seam allowance
- 1 separating zipper, of the length of the jacket including the turtleneck length and seam allowance

How to do it

Place the sweater flat onto a table and mark the front center with pins, then mark the front center with a basting line.

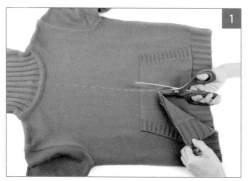

Cut the sweater along the basting line.

Here's the sweater completely cut open.

Place the ribbon along the front edge, with half its width extending off the edge. Allow ⅜" extra at the top of the collar and at the waistband. Pin, and stitch the ribbon on.

Fold under the ⅜" seam allowances at the top and bottom. Fold the extra ribbon width to the inside, and stitch it in place from the right side (stitching in the ditch of your first row).

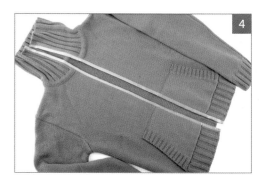

This is how the finished stitched ribbon looks.

Place one zipper piece under the edge and stitch so it is hidden. Fold the zipper ends under at the upper edge. Repeat with the other piece on the other side.

Wild but Harmless

Is the collar worn out from washing? With a new scarf-style collar in a contrasting color, a blouse gets a makeover.

Materials

- one blouse
- ½ yard polyester chiffon, 44" wide (for all sizes)

How to do it

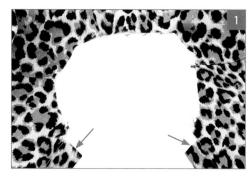

First, remove the collar. Fold under the seam allowances at the upper and lower flap (see arrows) and sew together by hand.

Fold the blouse along the center back. Pin the shoulder seams and front center together, and fold the neckline at the seam line, not at the cutting edge. Measure to the front center.

Cut the chiffon to size (see diagram on page 62): fold it in half lengthwise. Align the long sides on top of each other and cut off the ends at a slant. From the fold, measure toward the right a distance of half the neckline's measurement and mark. Mark the center back also.

Right sides together, align the scarf collar's lengthwise edges, and sew to the marks. Secure the seam at the ends. Trim the seam allowances

at the slanted ends. Turn the scarf right side out and iron the edges flat. Cut the neckline's seam allowance close to the seam.

Right sides together, sew the scarf collar onto the neckline. (Check for the mark at the back center.)

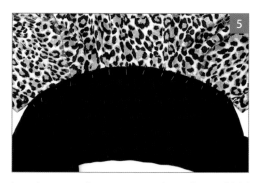

Iron the seam allowances into the collar, and fold the inner seam allowance and pin to the seam. Sew along the edge by hand.

Cool Combination

In the case of a T-shirt, you can do pretty much anything for the loop collar. It will always look great.

Materials

- one T-shirt
- ½ yard printed viscose (rayon) crepe, 44" wide

Loop Collar Pattern

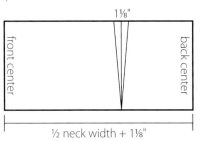

front center — back center

1⅛"

½ neck width + 1⅛"

How to do it

Fold the the T-shirt in half along the front center, pin the shoulder seams together, and place flat on a table.

Transfer the pattern for the loop collar onto paper.

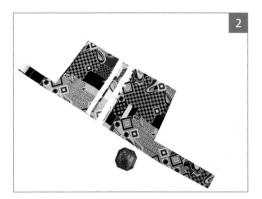

Measure the neckline with a measuring tape and use that measurement on the pattern, to mark the pattern's length.

Cut out the collar: place the fabric piece's edges toward the center then fold the fabric at the upper edge. Place the pattern pieces at the front and back center and pin them. Cut, adding on ⅜" of seam allowance.

Open the cut pieces and sew the side seams, right sides together. Iron the seam allowances open and iron toward the center.

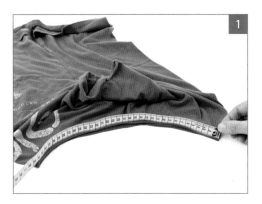

The assembled collar. ▶

Place the collar along the T-shirt neckline, right sides together, and stitch along the edge.

Pull out the other edge of the collar, pin it to the seam with the ⅜" of seam allowance folded under, and topstitch it along the seam, close to the edge.

Those jeans have stains that can't be removed? Don't throw them away, because you can make a miniskirt out of them in no time!

Materials

- one pair jeans
- heavy thread in orange (or matching the contrast color of the seams of the jeans)

How to do it

First, measure the intended length of the skirt.

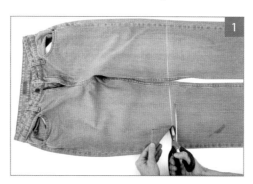

Transfer the skirt's length including 1⅜" for the hem onto the jeans, mark with chalk, and cut off.

Now rip out the inner leg seams. A tip: if you grab the end of the loosened thread and pull on it, the seam can be easily opened.

With the inner leg seams now unstitched, open the crotch seam at the front to the beginning of the zipper and at the back to the middle of the seam.

Place the front and back pieces on top of each other, and pin or baste them together. Topstitch the seams following the old seams exactly. Trim the seam allowance. Iron the hem edge to the inside, and topstitch it.

Fake Fur as Frost Protection!

Once there was an old jean jacket, which was transformed into a great winter vest. You'll only need some fluffy fake fur.

Materials

- one jean jacket
- ½ yard fake fur, 60" wide

How to do it

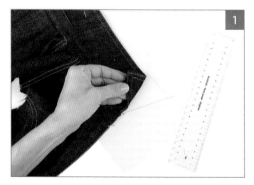

Carefully remove the sleeves from the jean jacket. Make a collar pattern: place the collar flat onto a piece of paper and pin it.

Trace along the collar's outer edge to the back center seam, and also mark the collar band's width. Turn around the paper with the collar pinned to it, and draw a line following the neck edge of the collar. Mark the location of the back center seam. Remove the paper and draw on the entire center seam. Cut out the pattern.

Make a pattern for the facing too.

Pin the pattern onto the fur and mark with chalk, adding ¼" at the neck only. Flip the pattern over and trace that onto the fur also.

Make sure the two pieces are drawn symmetrically.

Cut along the chalk marks. Try to only cut the fabric with the scissors—pull the fur fibers apart.

Pull the scraps away from the fur pieces. ▶

Right sides together, topstitch the collar pieces together along the back center. Carefully push back the fur fibers with the tip of the scissors.

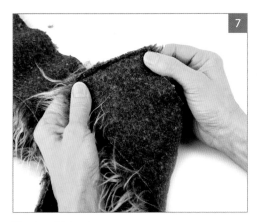

The topstitched seam…

…is invisible from the outside.

Fold the seam allowances of the armhole openings toward the inside and topstitch them. Place the prepared collar edging into the vest from the inside, and pin from the outside.

Pin the collar too. Then topstitch everything.

Cut strips for the armhole openings: 1⅛" wide, and the length of the sleeve openings. Topstitch the strips into the sleeve openings.

Stripes Meet Lace

A knit skirt gets some delicate lace ruffles. A strip of jersey of matching color is added to lengthen the garment.

Materials

• one jersey skirt
• jersey fabric for lengthening, 44" wide; length depends on the amount of lengthening you want to do (here: 4")
• ruffled lace trim, 4¾" wide; length is the width of the skirt hem taking into account the additional width of the skirt's stretching.

How to do it

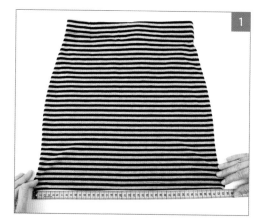

Place the skirt flat onto a table and measure the skirt seam—measure it while slightly stretched.

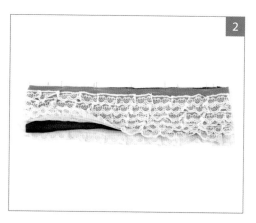

Cut the jersey strips and lace, adding ¾" of seam allowance. Iron the seam allowances open. Pin the lace onto the jersey strips and baste.

Tuck the ruffle under the skirt's hem seam, pin, and topstitch with a stretch stitch or a zigzag stitch.

Sleeveless Chic

This long-sleeved blouse is too warm, plus a sleeve is ripped. No problem, that can be fixed creatively!

Materials

- one blouse
- satin bias binding tape in contrasting color, ½" wide, approx. 1⅔ yard. The length depends on the size of the sleeve opening and the collar.

How to do it

First, to determine the length of the bias tape, measure one of the sleeve openings, double its measurement, and measure the collar edge. Carefully remove the sleeves with a seam ripper.

Partially pick out the tops of the side seams.

Cut off the seam allowance of the sleeve openings at the seam line.

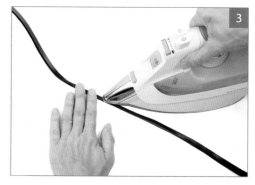

Iron the bias tape in half (if your bias tape isn't prefolded).

Place the cut edge of the sleeve opening into the fold of the bias tape and pin. Topstitch the bias tape closely along its edge. Hold the sleeve opening carefully so it stays in shape. Do the other sleeve opening in the same way.

Pick out the collar edge seams to reflect your preferred design. Cut off the seam allowance, and topstitch the bias tape on just as you did above. Fold the seam allowance of the bias tape under at the collar opening. Finally, sew the sections of unstitched side seams together again and flatten the seam allowances.

Blue Mood

This blazer is kind of awkward; the collar really doesn't cut it anymore. A cardigan offers more stylish options.

Materials
• one blazer

How to do it
Put on the blazer, or place it on a tailor's dummy.

Turn up the collar and baste the intended new line, i.e., along the dart line.

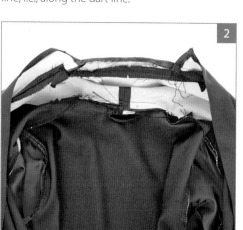

Rip out the seam at the back neck opening.

Completely remove the collar.

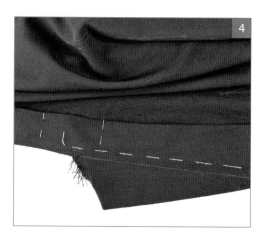

Pin the lapel facing against the front section, draw a line ⅜" next to the basting line… ▶

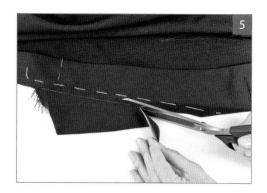

...and cut off the lapel.

Here's the finished cut neckline edge.

Fold the blazer along the back center line, and copy the neckline curve onto paper. Also measure the shoulder width of the front facing and make a facing pattern for the back piece.

Cut the facing for the back piece from the removed collar.

Topstitch the back facing's ends to the front facings, right sides together. Fold the seam allowance inside and topstitch.

Then place the facing on the piece, right sides together, and topstitch around the lapels and neckline.

Cut off the excess seam allowance and slightly notch it at the back neckline. Fold the seam allowances toward the facing and topstitch, close to the seam. The seam allowances are underneath.

Flatten the edges with an iron.

If you want you can add darts to the waist—front and back.

Brand New Frill

Almost everybody has a white blouse in the closet. You can quickly turn it into a special piece with frills and a standup collar.

Materials

- a white blouse
- 3¼ yards white satin ribbon, 1" wide
- 6½ yards white satin ribbon, 1½" wide
- 22 yards fusible bias tape, ¼" wide

How to do it

Remove any pockets if necessary.

Multiply the desired frill length three times, adding 1⅛" seam allowance. For example, if your planned final length for the finished frill is 12", that makes 37⅛" including 1⅛" of seam allowance. If your finished frill will be 10", that makes 31½" including 1⅛" of seam allowance.

Cut two pieces each of narrow and wide ribbon to that length, for the front frill. Cut 1 piece of wide ribbon for the collar.

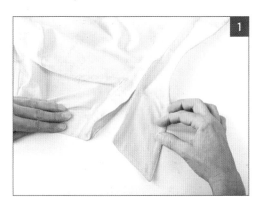

Use a seam ripper to open the seam at the base of the collar, then remove the collar from the blouse.

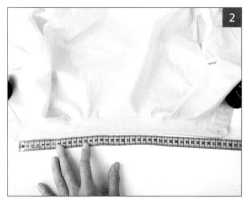

Measure the collar width at the base from the front, center to front center: here 15" x 1⅛" = 16⅞", including 1⅛" of seam allowance.

Iron the bias tape onto each edge of the satin ribbons. ▶

Starting ⅝" from the end, fold the wide ribbon toward the inside, and pin pleats in place, to create ¾"-wide box pleats.

Iron the collar frill into the open collar and topstitch the collar edges together again.

Iron on the second narrow frill along the bottom placket, and topstitch close to the edge.

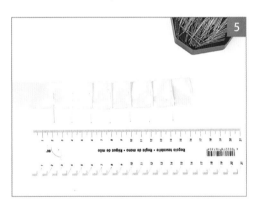

Fold the narrow ribbon into ¾"-wide box pleats.

Iron on the narrow frill tucking its edge under the top placket's edge.

Iron on the wide frills ⅝" apart, and topstitch close to the edge.

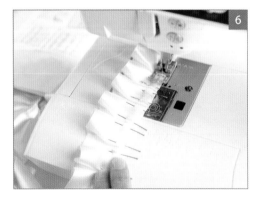

Topstitch the pleats.

Then topstitch close to the edge.

Top of the Line

An old skirt becomes a festive statement with lace godets. A lace finish at the hem is a particularly nice touch.

Materials

- one skirt
- lace, approx. 19¾" wide, 10" long

How to do it

Copy the pattern for the godet section (page 62) onto paper.

If there is a walking slit in your skirt, first close it with a stitch. Place the skirt flat onto a table and mark the front center at the hem with a pin.

Divide that length in half and mark the center.

Placing the measuring tape straight at the hem, measure 7⅞" toward the top and mark the spot. For the second godet, mark the same spot on the other half of the front piece.

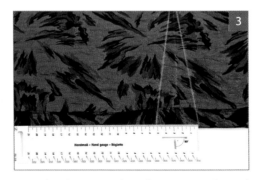

Turn the skirt around to the wrong side, and

mark the center line. Measure 1" from the hem to each side. Connect those dots with the top of the center line so a wedge is formed.

Cut out the wedge, first adding on ⅜" along the lines. Carefully cut toward the wedge's point, stopping just before the mark.

Place the godet pattern onto the lace and cut out the piece. Repeat for the second godet.

Pin the godet pieces to the skirt and topstitch from the hem to the corner with a short stitch. Lockstitch to secure the seam, and then topstitch up the other side.

Smooth the stitched edges, fold the lace at the seam toward the inside, and stitch.

All Laced Up

An invitation to a party? No outfit seems appropriate? This T-shirt looks just as great with jeans as it does with a maxi skirt.

Materials

- one T-shirt
- ⅓ yard tulle lace, 44" wide
- jersey fabric (remnant), approx. 28" wide, 2" long

How to do it

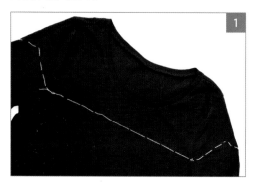

Mark a line at the T-shirt where you want the yoke line to be. You can choose whether the lace yoke will be at the front section only or at the back section as well. The sleeve has a lateral marking at the lace edge (see photo). Pin a piece of paper onto the front and back sections. Do likewise at the sleeve. Fold the yoke pattern at the center and even out the sleeve and neck opening. Cut out your patterns.

Fold the lace in half and pin on the patterns. Cut the pieces to size. Only add a seam allowance of ⅜" at the sleeve opening and at the shoulder seam.

Place the front and back pieces right sides together and topstitch one of the shoulder seams. Iron the seam allowance toward the back.
Measure the neck opening and cut a 1⅛"-wide strip of that length from the jersey fabric. Careful: cut the jersey strip crosswise to the stretch! Trim the neck opening with the strip.

Topstitch the other shoulder seam right sides together, serge the seam allowances, and iron toward the back. Secure the seam allowance at the shoulder. Then add the sleeve sections.

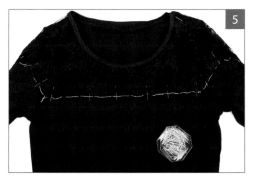

Now place the finished lace yoke along the basting line of the T-shirt. Make sure the seams of the sleeve openings of the T-shirt and the yoke are aligned on top of each other. Pin. Topstitch with a small zigzag stitch right along the lace's edge.

Turn the T-shirt inside out and cut the excess T-shirt fabric away close to the zigzag line.

Once There Was a Shirt...

An old light blue men's shirt can be quickly transformed into a feminine casual top with a waistband.

Materials

- one men's shirt
- white elastic, 2" wide, the length of the hip measurement

How to do it

Put on the shirt and mark off the extra width at the side seams. Place the elastic at the appropriate height and mark. Then baste the line.

Mark ⅝" along the new side seam as seam allowance, then cut off the extra fabric.

Cut back the upper seam allowance to ¼".

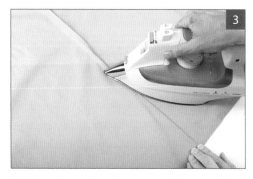

Fold and iron the other seam allowance. Topstitch close to the edge.

At the front section, measure 4" from the front edge to each side and mark with a basting thread. Place the elastic around your waist and keep it stretched. Measure the length, adding ⅜" of seam allowance for each side. Cut the elastic, fold in half, and mark the center. Also mark the back center of the shirt. On the wrong side, pin the elastic to the back center and pin it at the front. Even out the extra length.

Topstitch the elastic while keeping it stretched. Topstitch two or three rows close to each other.

Smart Lengthening!

That old skirt is too short? With two or more elegant flounces made from taffeta, it's transformed to the length you want.

Materials
- one skirt
- ⅔ to ¾ yard polyester taffeta, 44" wide

How to do it

Draw the patterns for the flounces from pages 62–63 onto paper. Draw two separate patterns (the inner cutting line = the narrower flounce).

Place the skirt flat onto a table and measure the front hem width. Turn the skirt around and measure the back hem width (adding the slit underlap, if the skirt has a slit).

Transfer the skirt's hem width to the longer edge of the patterns. Careful: the flounce patterns correspond to only a quarter of the skirt's hem width!

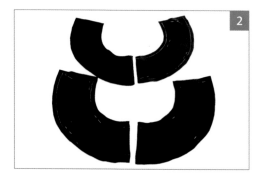

Place the sections onto the taffeta so one straight side lies at the fold of the fabric, then pin. Cut 2 of each flounce.

Sew together the long edges of the wide flounce pieces, right sides together. Repeat for the narrow flounce pieces. Trim the seam allowances and iron open. Topstitch the hem edge.

Place the wide flounce ⅜" under the skirt's hem and pin. Topstitch from the right side, very closely along the edge.

Measure 1" up from the skirt's hem and baste a line. Place the narrow flounce onto the basting line facing up, and topstitch. Carefully iron it flat toward the bottom.

Chinos—Cool and Classic

Some like it fast! For an upcycle that's simple and finished in almost no time, transform a pair of wide leg pants into chinos.

Materials

• one pair of wide leg pants

How to do it

Put on the pants and pin them to your desired leg width; pin along the inside and outside seams.

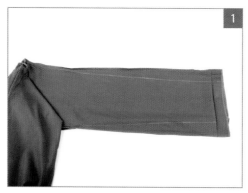

Pin through only the top (front) fabric layer. Turn the pants inside out. Unpick the hem, and mark the pinned line with chalk. Remove the pins and draw a solid line.

Prepare the other leg the same way. Stitch along the lines. Cut the seams' edges back to ⅜" and trim.

Shorten the pants as needed, or roll them up.

Adorned with Feathers

So that sweater is boring? With this marabou feather boa, it'll become a new standout.

Materials

- one sweater
- marabou feather boa, available by the yard. The length depends on the size of the neck opening and the cuffs.

How to do it

First, measure around the neckline and the cuff width. Careful: double the width of the cuff.

Loosely pin the feather boa along the neckline, then cut to length.

Sew on the feather boa by hand. This is best done from the wrong side so that the feathers are not caught in the thread.

Do the same with the cuffs.

For the Figure's Sake

The skirt is too tight, and its seam allowance isn't sufficient to make it wider? Adding panels of knit fabric will make it fit.

Materials

- one skirt
- tubular ribbing, approx. 19¾" wide, depending on the skirt's length (here: 23⅝")
- waistband, 1⅛" wide, the length of the waist plus the seam allowance
- 1 skirt hook-and-eye closure

How to do it

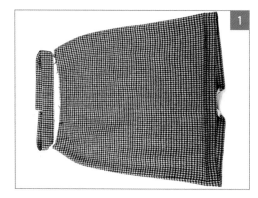

Remove the waistband from the skirt. Pick out the hem. If the skirt has a slit, topstitch it closed.

Mark the skirt's length, including the hem and upper seam allowance, on the tubular ribbing.

Mark the width of the strip on the fabric tube: for size 4 and 6 = 4¾", for size 8 and 10 = 5½", for size 12 and 14 = 6¼".

Take ⅝" for the waist arch at the waist line of one of the sides into account (see arrow) so the seam allowance of the side seam gets wider at the waist.

Rip out the side seams (of the lining fabric too if applicable).

Pin the lining and outer fabric together. Mark the width of the ribbing strip (4¾", 5½", or 6¼")—approximately ¾" more at the front than at the back section. See photo: 2¾" at the front, 2" at the back. Baste the lines with a thread.

Cut off the excess fabric ⅜" away from the basting thread.

Pin the ribbing strip to the skirt right sides together.

Topstitch both sides and trim the seam allowance.

Iron the seam allowances toward the skirt fabric, and topstitch from the right side close to the edge of the skirt fabric. Fold the hem to the inside, iron it, and stitch by hand.

Measure the waist width and add ⅜" of seam allowance for the underlap and 2" for the overlap.

Cut the waistband to that length and pin to the edge of the waist.

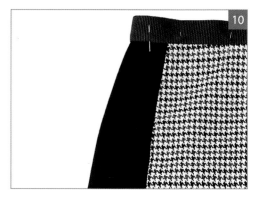

If the waist of the skirt is too wide, work the extra width of the knitwear into a dart (approx. 4–4¾" long). Topstitch the waistband close to the edge. Iron the waistband to the inside, at the back center fold the seam allowance to the inside, leave 1" at the overlap, and sew on the hook and eyelet.

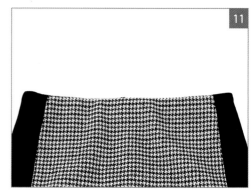

This is the finished waist.

It'll Be a Hot Summer

An old men's jacket, too nice to give away! The solution: off with the sleeves—and there's your new outfit.

Materials

• one men's jacket

How to do it

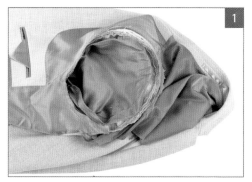

Remove the sleeve lining and shoulder pads and cut off the sleeves.

This is the sleeve opening with sleeve removed.

If necessary, make the blazer tighter at the side seams so the sleeve openings get smaller as well.

Turn under the sleeve opening edges and the lining edges, tucking the seam allowances to the inside, and topstitch the front half of the sleeve opening from the right side. Do likewise with the back half of the sleeve opening. Iron the sleeve opening edges flat. If the blazer has no lining, finish the turned over edge with bias tape.

Old jeans are still useful! Just cut off the legs and roll up the hem to make hot pants.

Materials

• **one pair of jeans**

How to do it

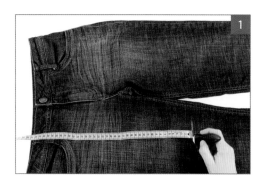

Measure the length you want for the hot pants from the upper waist band edge. Include 3⅛" for rolling up the hem.
Mark a line with chalk.

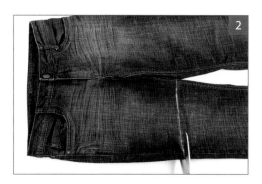

Cut off the leg along the chalk line.

Fold the cut leg onto the other leg and cut along the edge, to make the second leg symmetrical.

Measure about 1⅝" from the bottom of the leg and mark.

Turn the edge up twice and topstitch at the side seams.

Color Block Update

Add two large colorful strips of jersey to it, and your T-shirt becomes a minidress.

Materials

- one T-shirt
- ½ yard yellow jersey, 44" wide
- ¼ yard patterned jersey, 44" wide

How to do it

Put the T-shirt on, or put it on a tailor's dummy. Use a measuring tape to determine the new length of the shirt. (The front should be a little longer.) Baste a line. Remove the trim at the neck opening. Cut off the shirt ⅜" below the basting line.

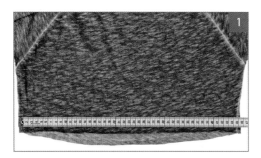

Measure the hem width at the front and back sections.

Cut the fabrics to size: top edge of the yellow jersey = T-shirt circumference plus ⅜" of seam allowance. Allow to widen toward the bottom by about 2⅜" on each side (including seam allowance). Check the waist width to make sure the skirt won't be too tight. Then cut the hem strip to the width of the yellow jersey.

Rip out a short section of the shirt's side seams and topstitch on the yellow skirt section, right sides together. Use an overlock machine or topstitch with a long zigzag stitch. Trim the seam allowance and iron it toward the top. Then topstitch on the hem strip, right sides together, and continue as described above.

Place the side seams together so the seam intersections match, then topstitch, trim, and iron flat. Topstitch the hem.

Rip out a section of the shoulder seam, measure the neckline, and cut a strip of 1⅝"-wide jersey of that length. Careful: cut the jersey strip crosswise to the stretch! Fold the strip in half lengthwise. Right sides together, topstitch the strip, slightly stretched, along the neck opening. Iron the seam allowance toward the inside, trim the edge, and topstitch from the right side close to the edge.

Last, close the section of shoulder seam. Shorten the sleeves as you wish.

Materials and Tools

Sewing machine needles

Their size depends on the fabric and the thread thickness you're using. Sewing machine manufacturers provide guidance charts. Generally, the higher the needle number the thicker the needle. In needle sizes like "80/12," the higher number measures the diameter in fractions of a millimeter; the lower number is the numbering system used in the US. Use thin needles for fine fabrics (60/8 or 70/10).

Pins and sewing needles

Pins are indispensable for securing fabric layers. And always keep a selection of general use needles handy to baste hand stitches.

Thread

Always make sure you purchase high-quality thread to avoid ripping, knots, loops, and jumping spools. Synthetic yarns are very durable, can sew pretty much anything, and are exceptionally good for beginners. There are also cotton or delicate silk yarns. Basting thread consists of loosely plied cotton, and can be easily broken and removed quickly.

Scissors, seam ripper

You need a pair of fabric scissors to cut the fabric. They should be used exclusively for this task. Use a second pair of scissors to cut out paper patterns. Seam rippers are very helpful to rip out sewing, or to dismantle clothing.

Measuring tape and chalk or fabric markers

A measuring tape is indispensable for cutting and sewing precisely. Tailor's chalk and water-soluble fabric markers are used to trace patterns onto fabrics and to mark lines. Chalk tends to brush off with time, but still, it is best used on the wrong side of the fabric. It's especially suitable for marking long cuts.

Sewing ABC

Box pleat

An inner pleat. It consists of two pleats butting into each other at the fold.

Chiffon

Delicate, semi-transparent fabric made from silk or synthetics.

Flounce

Wide, circular-shaped and folded edging, e.g., on a skirt or dress.

Fold

A pattern usually shows a fold by using a dotted line. Fold the fabric and place the corresponding edge of the pattern along the fold, without seam allowance. There is no seam created here.

Gathering

Stitch two rows about ¼" apart along an edge, using large stitches. Leave a long thread at the beginning and at the end of the row; don't lockstitch to secure the stitches. By pulling the lower threads, the fabric can now be gathered. Pull the fabric into gathers as shown. Once the piece has the desired width, secure the stitches with a knot and even out the gathers.

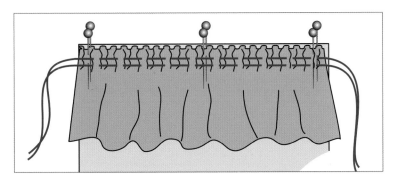

Gore

A wedge-shaped fabric insert placed into the hem of a skirt to widen it.

Jersey

A general term for many kinds of knit fabric. See Knitwear

Knitwear

To make knitwear using fabrics like jersey or velour, it's best to use a special jersey needle. Some sewing machines offer a jersey stitch, as well.

Lockstitching

At the beginning and end of every seam, make a few stitches forward and then backward so the seam doesn't come undone. Sew three to four stitches when starting, push the reverse button/switch, and sew three to four stitches before advancing once again. Secure the end of the seam with three to four backward stitches.

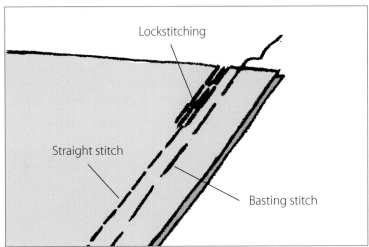

Lockstitching

Straight stitch

Basting stitch

Notching

At edges and round sections, the seam allowance is cut in triangular snips to near the seam line. This allows for the seams to lie flat.

Pinning and basting

Always secure fabric pieces with pins and with long running hand stitches or with a sewing machine's long straight stitches, so they do not slip or fold. Always place pins crosswise and remove them one by one when sewing so the sewing machine needle doesn't break.

Right and wrong sides of fabrics

Every fabric has a right side and a wrong side. The right side corresponds to the outer side. In the case of printed fabrics, the pattern is clearly visible. If fabrics are placed right sides together, the outer sides lie inside and the (less attractive) wrong sides lie outside. If fabrics are wrong sides together, the right sides lie outside.

Ruffle

A strip of fabric with varyingly wide gathering used to adorn edges such as hems, sleeves, or collars. See Gathering

Satin

Fabric with a very smooth, shiny surface. The term refers to the weave; satin can be made of cotton, silk, synthetic fibers, and blends.

Seam allowance

The fabric betweeen the edge and the seam. If the fabric is sewn too close to the edge the seam will rip open, so a seam allowance is added to the pattern. Its width is always indicated.

Seam intersections

Place the seams precisely on top of each other at the intersection. Cut away the edges of the seam allowance so they taper.

Use an iron to open the seam allowances. The seams intersect at right angles on the right side of the fabric.

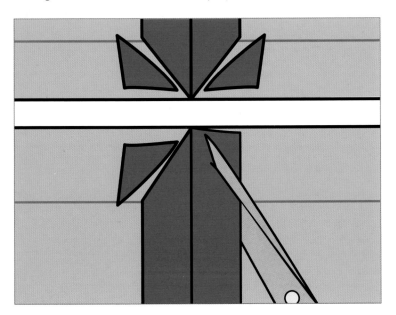

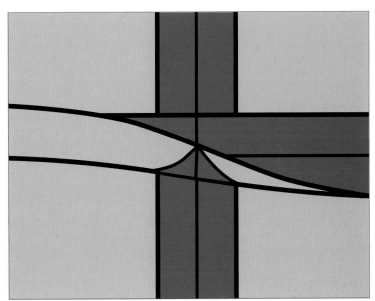

First, pin the fabric pieces at the intersection, then pin the remaining seam and baste. Stitch as a simple seam.

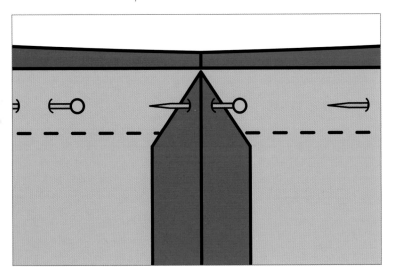

Stitching

Use the sewing machine with the regular, straight stitch setting.

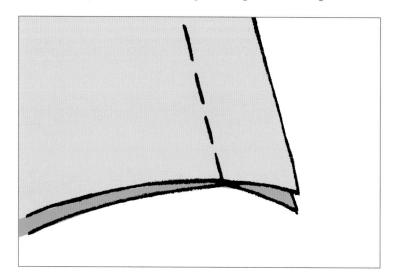

Stitching close to the edge

For stitching close to the edge the needle is barely ⅛"away from the fabric edge or fold.

Stitching in the ditch

Stitch as closely as possible to the seam on the right side.

Taffeta

Shiny, stiff fabric consisting of silk or synthetics (e.g., polyester taffeta).

Thread tension

Depending on the type of fabric, the thread tension of the machine must be adjusted so loops are avoided. It's best to sew a small test piece to check the tension.

Trimming

In order to avoid the fraying of the fabric edges the seam allowances should be trimmed. The zigzag or overlock stitch is suitable. If you trim the two seam allowances of a seam separately, do it before performing the stitch.

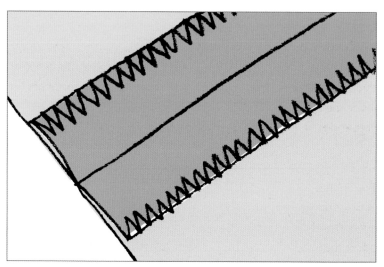

The seam allowances are trimmed together once the seam has been closed.

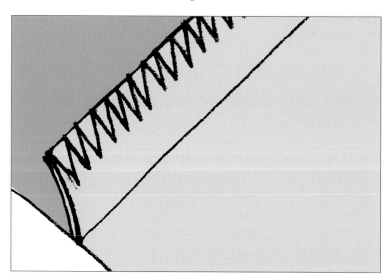

Turning right side out

Two pieces of fabric (e.g., for a collar) are sewn right sides together, and then turned right side out so that the right side of the fabric is outside and the seam allowances become invisible between the pieces of fabric.

Upper and lower threads

Each sewing machine stitch consists of an upper and a lower thread. The upper thread, from the spool, is guided from the top of the machine through various guides to the needle. The lower thread is from a bobbin inside the bobbin case below the needle plate. Before stitching, the lower thread must be drawn up onto the needle plate.

Upper flap and lower flap (extension)

Two finished edges which overlap. The upper flap is always on top, the lower flap is underneath. Such overlapping fabric pieces—a skirt slit, a closing edge, etc.—are often reinforced with interfacing. In the case of buttoned edges, the upper flap is usually fitted with buttonholes, and the lower flap is used to attach the buttons.

Zigzag stitch

Use this setting for sewing elastic or any stretch fabrics (e.g., jersey).

Patterns

Godet Pattern, Skirt with godet, page 36

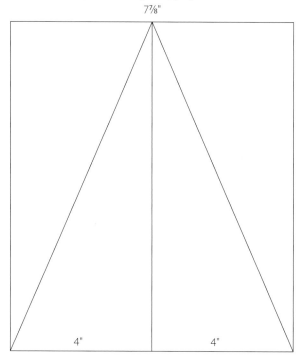

7⅞"

4"   4"

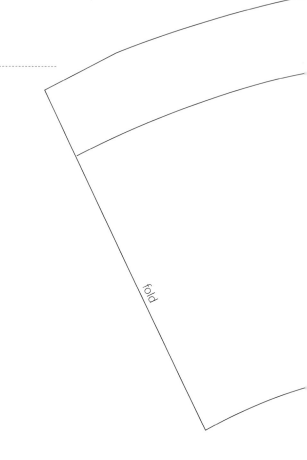

fold

Collar Pattern, Scarf-collar blouse, page 18

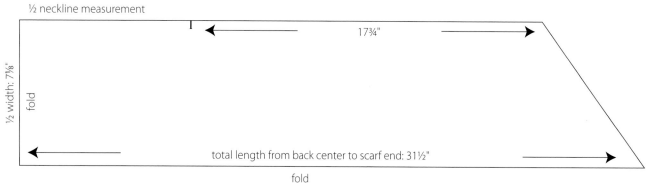

½ neckline measurement

½ width: 7⅛"

fold

17¾"

fold

total length from back center to scarf end: 31½"

fold

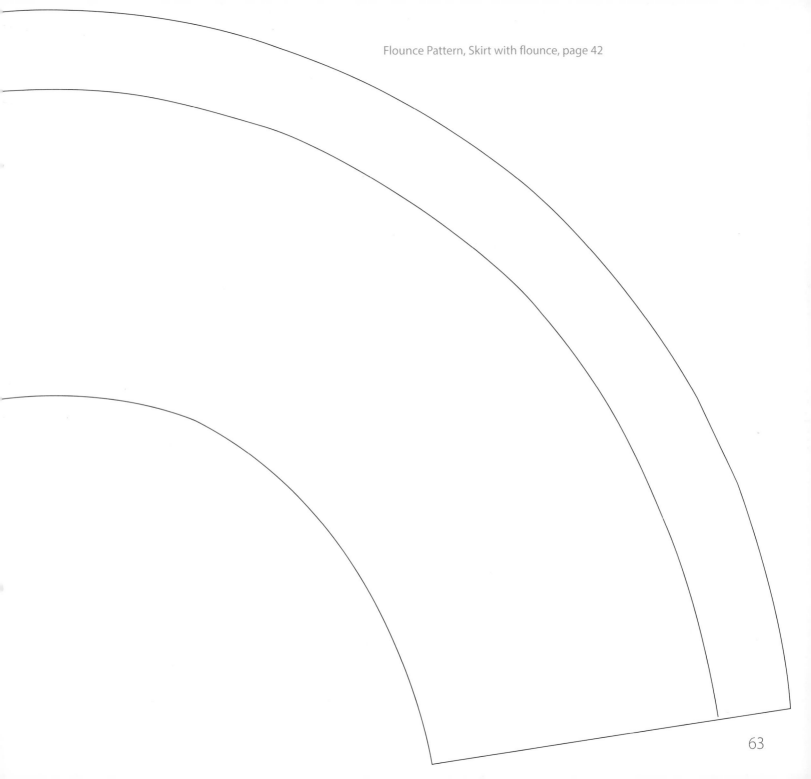

Other Schiffer Books on Related Subjects:

Fun Felt Crafts: Penny Rugs & Pretty Things from Recycled Wool by Tina Skinner, ISBN 978-0-7643-3299-9

High Fashion Handbags: Classic Vintage Designs by Adrienne Astrologo & Nancy Schiffer, ISBN 978-0-7643-2508-3

International Steampunk Fashions by Victoriana Lady Lisa, ISBN 978-0-7643-4207-3

Library of Congress Control Number: 2015934571

Originally published as *Aus Alt näh Neu!* by Christophorus Verlag GmbH & Co. KG, Freiburg © Christophorus Verlag GmbH & Co. KG, 2013.

Translated from the German by Jonee Tiedemann.

Cover designed by Brenda McCallum
Type set in Gabriola/Myriad Pro

ISBN: 978-0-7643-4849-5
Printed in China

Published by Schiffer Publishing, Ltd.
4880 Lower Valley Road
Atglen, PA 19310
Phone: (610) 593-1777; Fax: (610) 593-2002
E-mail: Info@schifferbooks.com

For our complete selection of fine books on this and related subjects, please visit our website at www.schifferbooks.com. You may also write for a free catalog.

This book may be purchased from the publisher. Please try your bookstore first.

We are always looking for people to write books on new and related subjects. If you have an idea for a book, please contact us at proposals@schifferbooks.com.

Schiffer Publishing's titles are available at special discounts for bulk purchases for sales promotions or premiums. Special editions, including personalized covers, corporate imprints, and excerpts can be created in large quantities for special needs. For more information, contact the publisher.

Design, concept, and text: Mia Führer

Photography: Florian Bilger

Styling: Peggy Kummerow

Step-by-step photos: Thorsten Klemz,

Andreas Lehmann

Patterns and templates: Mia Führer

Design: GrafikwerkFreiburg